# The Dolphin
# Who Loves Golfin'!

By Pete Shoemaker

Illustrated by Karen Donovan Matchette

Along the California shore,
Where dolphins swim and seagulls soar,
There is a city—and a bay—
That we all know as Monterey.

A lovely place, this coastal town,
Where people come from all around
To marvel how the land and sea
Can meet in such sweet harmony.

Golfers love to come and play

The great golf courses by the bay,

And they're in heaven when they reach

The golf course known as Pebble Beach.

And here, beyond the 18th tee
Is where our story starts, you see.

The 18th hole runs all the way

Along a cliff above the bay.

Golfers love the ocean view,

But it can make them nervous, too.


No matter where those golf balls go

There's ocean not too far below!

And if the shots those golfers hit

Are crooked just a little bit,

Guess where those golf balls soon will be?

You're right! **Ka-SPLASH!** Right in the sea!

Sinking slowly—down, down, down—

Where whales and dolphins swim around.

Yes, dolphins live within the bay
Just off the coast of Monterey.

They like to swim and
sing and spout
And jump and spin and flip about.

So in big boats all through the day
People watched the dolphins play.

But one brave dolphin, very small,

Loved the people most of all.

And this most eager, friendly one,

Was the youngest dolphin — Don.

Now Don would try—oh how he would!—
To do what older dolphins could,
When they would take their airborne trips
And do their special double flips!

Double flips! You heard me right—
Twice around in just one flight!

The people in the boats would cheer,
And that's the sound Don longed to hear.

But there was just one little blip;
Don couldn't **DO** a double flip.

He'd try and try with all his might,
But couldn't seem to get it right.

One sunny day a giant ship
On a whale-and-dolphin trip,

Filled with folks—above, below—
Came looking for the dolphin show.

All Don needed was one glance
To know this was his biggest chance!

So down he dove—way, way, down deep—
Then turned and swam with all his speed,
And shooting upwards, at the top
Did one flip and then...**Ka-FLOP!**

He hit the water with a sound

That people heard for miles around!

Water splashed up in the air

As people howled everywhere,

Pointing, laughing, hands on knees —

The funniest thing they'd ever seen!

Off he swam, filled with disgrace,
Tears of shame upon his face.

**"I'm a failure! I'm no good!"**
**I'll never do it — never could!"**

Racing, plunging, diving on,
All alone — poor dolphin Don!

Could this be how his story ends—
Far from family and friends?

It seemed like all was lost that day,

But all was not, I'm glad to say!

The sun shone brightly in the sky.

The ocean sparkled in reply.

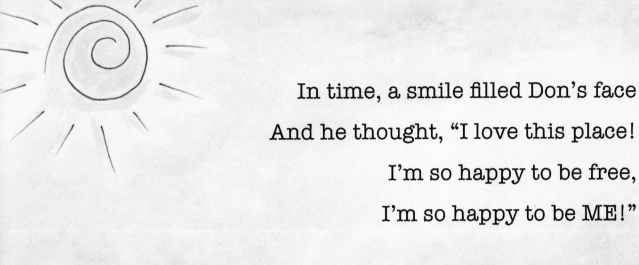

In time, a smile filled Don's face
And he thought, "I love this place!
I'm so happy to be free,
I'm so happy to be ME!"

And so the joy he felt arise

Sent him soaring in the sky,

Flipping over twice and then

Smoothly diving back again.

**A double flip!** With grace and style—
The kind to make you cheer and smile!
Don had done it, then and there!
No one saw—he didn't care!

Then suddenly, to his surprise —

A wondrous vision met his eyes!

People, people, everywhere!

Crowds of them from here to there.

Hundreds, thousands, maybe more
Along the cliff above the shore!

It just so happened, on that day,

To Pebble Beach had come to play

The greatest golfers, far and wide,

Competing for a golden prize.


And at that moment, don't you know,

The match was on the final hole.

One golfer was the favorite
And oh! the shot that he'd just hit.
He'd reached the green in two, you see,
Just one foot from an eagle three!

And now the other had to play—
The local pro from Monterey.

He knew then, as he eyed the pin,

He'd need a miracle to win.

He took a breath, the club went back,

The crowd roared as they heard the crack.

The ball soared up into its flight

But then—oh no!—an awful sight:

It started sailing wide and free

**Heading out into the sea!**

Ten thousand mouths dropped open wide
Letting out ten thousand sighs.
Ten thousand pairs of eyes just stared
As the ball flew through the air.

But watching where the ball had gone,
The crowd was looking right at Don!

Don didn't even see the ball.

He saw ten thousand looks—that's all.

He first was scared, then got a grip:

He had to do a **TRIPLE flip!**

So down he dove, way, way down deep,
Then turned and swam with all his speed,
And shooting upwards, curved his back...

Was it luck—now was that all—
That made Don's tail fin hit that ball?

We don't know that, but this we do:
Back from the sea that golf ball flew.

As thousands turned their heads in shock,
The ball fell on the green....**Ka-PLOP!**

And bounded swiftly up and up

And up and up
**Into the Cup!**

The crowd exploded with a cheer
That people miles away could hear!

They jumped, they yelled, they clapped their hands,
They hugged each other, tossed their hats!
They laughed and pointed out to sea
And waved their arms hysterically!

Yes, Don had found the perfect way
To make folks happy every day.
And now, he saves the golfers' shots
And flips them to the perfect spots!

# Fin

His exploits by the oceanside
Have made him famous far and wide.
Of all the dolphins he, by far,
Is the biggest, brightest star!

HE'S A GOLF
PHENOMENON!

PLAYING
TO THE
CROWD

'S NATURAL
NG ANALYZED

Spouts
Illustrated

DOLPHIN
STAR AT
PEBBLE
BEACH

BLOWS THEM
OUT OF THE
WATER

And so, the moral of our tale
Is one where joy and hope prevail.

For if you follow what's inside,
And let your joy become your guide,
You'll find that who you really are
Is a brightly shining star!

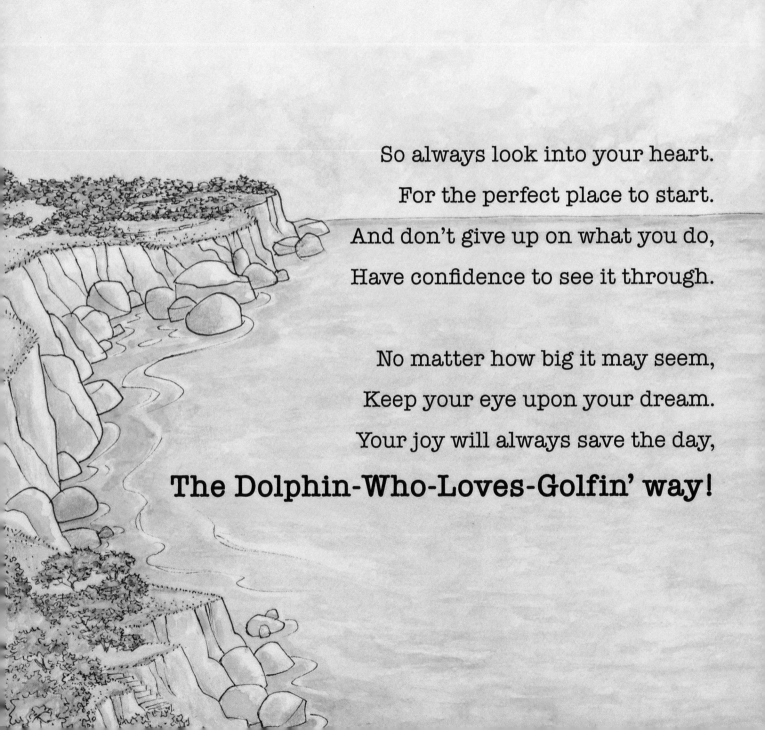

So always look into your heart.

For the perfect place to start.

And don't give up on what you do,

Have confidence to see it through.


No matter how big it may seem,

Keep your eye upon your dream.

Your joy will always save the day,

**The Dolphin-Who-Loves-Golfin' way!**

ISBN: 978-1-54397-777-6

Written by Pete Shoemaker
Illustrated by Karen Donovan Matchette

Book Design by Leslie Taylor
Buffalo Creative Group | buffalocreativegroup.com